GW00498913

is book are prayers for those called to minister...

DICTIONARY DEFINITIONS:

Calling: a strong urge towards a particular way of life; a voca
Synonyms: vocation, mission; call, summ

Ministry: the spiritual work or service of a Christian or a g
of Christians. The action of ministering to some
Synonyms: teaching, preaching, evange

The dictionary definitions of calling and ministry don't
justice to the full concepts behind the words.

A CALLING is doing what you have a passi
for, doing what you love with a sense of
rightness.

MINISTRY is doing what God has called yo
to do, it is any action, work or activity tha
helps others to know God better.

Each of us has a call to minister to others

*Carry each other's burdens, and in this way
you will fulfill the law of Christ. (Gal. 6:2)*

*Therefore, I urge you, brothers and sisters, in view
God's mercy, to offer your bodies as a living sacrifi
holy and pleasing to God—this is your true and pro
worship. (Rom. 12:1)*

**Listen - hear your call.
Act - as God directs.
Pray - talk with God.
Be - the person God created you to be.**

HELP ME DEAR LORD

TO CARE TOO MUCH

TO LOVE TOO FREELY

TO PRAY UNCEASINGLY

TO FORGIVE ENDLESSLY

TO LAUGH FEARLESSLY

TO QUESTION

TO LIVE

TO BE WHO I AM

TO BE WHERE I AM

TO BE WHAT I AM

TO HOPE

TO BELIEVE

TO REACH OUT
MY
HAND

MORNING PRAYERS

*Breathe slowly and deeply whilst looking at the flame
of a candle, a cross or a suitable image.*

Creator God I give this time to You.

Jesus teach me how to love,
How to live in Your presence.
Jesus teach me how to live,
How to pray in Your will.
Jesus teach me how to pray,
How to rest in Your embrace.
Jesus teach me how to rest,
How to be in Your world.
Jesus teach me how to be,
How to love in Your way.

*Create a pure heart in me, O God, and put
a new and loyal spirit in me. (Psalm 51)*

As I breathe in -   I give thanks for the coming day.
As I breathe out - I place into Your hands
the things I do.
As I breathe in -   I ask for Your blessing
on those who love You.
As I breathe out - I pray for Your blessing
on those who don't know You.

y each moment today be filled with light,
y each challenge today be met with grace,
y each choice today follow Your plan,
d may I sense Your wondrous presence in all things.

Grant me times today,
> Times of stillness,
>> Spreading like ripples on water.

> May Your peace fill me.

Grant me times today,
> Times of laughter,
>> That transform today.

> May Your joy sustain me.

Grant me times today,
> Times of blessing,
>> Feeding my soul.

> May Your love surround me.

Create a pure heart in me, O God,
and put a new and loyal spirit in me.
(Psalm 51)

Do not banish me from Your presence;
not take Your Holy Spirit away from me.
(Psalm 51)

Make a circling action around yourself
as you say the words 'Circle me'.

God of all **circle me**,
Protect me as I travel
through today.

God of all **circle me**,
Grant me the blessings
of Your mercy.

God of all **circle me**,
Refresh my spirit
and soften my heart.

Let my eyes see as You see,
with compassion and love for others.
Let my ears hear as You hear,
with a soft heart and love for others.
Let my feet dare to walk,
with Your purpose for this world.
Let my hands ache to work,
with Your direction in this world.

In the early moments of this day...

I pray wisdom for our leaders,
I pray peace where there is conflict,
I pray hope where there is despair,
I pray joy where there is sorrow,
I pray love where there is hate.

MIDDAY quick PRAYER

In the midst of this day
let me not be so busy,
That Your voice is lost.

In the midst of this day
let me not be so tired,
That Your will is not done.

In the midst of this day
let me find peace,
And time to just be.

ENING PRAYERS

the slowly and deeply whilst looking at the flame
candle, a cross or a suitable image.

breathe in -   I give thanks for a day well ended.
I reflect on each little moment
of joy and learning.
Bless me as I give You thanks.

breathe out - I place into Your hands
the things unfinished,
May they not become a burden.
Bless me as I praise You.

On the wars and rumours of wars,
Shine Your light.
On the poor and the oppressed,
Shine Your light.
On the disasters and terrible things,
Shine Your light.

Shine Your light on my path, may I follow Your way.
Shine Your light in my darkness, may I know Your love.
Shine Your light on my face, may I reflect Your glory

Lord, help me to serve.
Help me to be Your Light.

As the waves of a calm sea
Lap gently on the shore,
      May Your Spirit bring us peace.

As the cool breeze on a Summer day
Caresses and refreshes,
      May Your peace bring us calm.

As the sweet songs of nature
Soothe our busy minds,
      May Your calm bring us peace.

*I will lie down and fall asleep in peace because
you alone, Lord, let me live in safety.
(Psalm 4:8)*

*Make a circling action around yourself
as you say the words 'Circle me'.*

God of all things, **circle me**,
    Protect me as I sleep.

God of small things, **circle me**,
    Grant me good sleep.

God of eternal things, **circle me**,
    Refresh me as I sleep.

no unpleasant thoughts or dreams disturb me,
my resting mind be filled with peace,
my aches and pains diminish,
troubles stay outside the door,
my sleep restore and strengthen me.

In the quiet before I rest
I thank You for today,
For the good,
For the difficult,
For the painful,
For the joyful.

In the darkness of this night
I pray for the dispossessed,
For the poor,
For the lonely,
For the lost,
For the sad.

In the last moments of this day...

I pray wisdom for our leaders,
I pray peace where there is conflict,
I pray hope where there is despair,
I pray joy where there is sorrow,
I pray love where there is hate.

CIRCLE ME THIS NIGHT
KEEP PEACE WITHIN
AND ANGER WITHOUT

CIRCLE ME THIS NIGHT
KEEP COMFORT WITHIN
AND HARDSHIP WITHOUT

CIRCLE MY HOME THIS NIGH
KEEP SAFETY WITHIN
AND DANGER WITHOUT

MY LIFE IS IN YOUR HAND:
HOLD ME GENTLY AS I RES